ABSTRACT

A finite automaton is abstractly represented as a
set function from one finite set into another. Many of
the problems posed for finite automata are then simply
described in terms of set functions with special properties.
Some elementary results on the existence and uniqueness of
such "discrimination functions" are presented.

As a related example a finite automaton is described
which can recognize a large variety of geometric patterns
(or characters) when displayed in a rather general way.

A finite automaton which is essentially a "perceptron"
is described. In order that such a device represent a
discrimination function it is shown that a specific
product of two set functions must also represent a
discrimination function. Some rather severe necessary
conditions for solving the basic discrimination problem
are then derived.

Some final comments on approximate discrimination
and generalizations of the basic formulation are given.

TABLE OF CONTENTS

FINITE AUTOMATA,
PATTERN RECOGNITION AND PERCEPTRONS

1. Introduction.

A large class of finite automata can be classified as devices which exhibit some type of selective responses to parts of their "environment". In addition many automata which are of current interest are intended to have definite similarities with, or to be in some sense analogous to human nervous systems (insofar as the latter are understood). The all too frequent overemphasis on these aspects of automata, with the subsequent morass of psychological and physiological terminology introduced, conceals the nature of the basic (mathematical) problem which must be considered. The first part of this paper (section 2) presents a formulation of the general problem posed by many automata, namely: to find a specific set function or class of set functions. The formulation presented can be easily extended to include a more general class of automata (or discrimination problems) than those explicitly considered; one such extension is discussed in Section 7.

The problem of "recognizing" geometric patterns by automata is considered in Section 3. A specific device which solves such problems with some generality is described. This example serves to yield insight into the formalities

(4)

introduced and discussed throughout the other sections of the paper. The principles of this automaton are so transparent that an anthropomorphic description of it, in such terms as "concept formation", "cognitive system", etc. is clearly not called for. However, if the device were described only by its function, and the simple trick of its operation were concealed, it would certainly qualify as an automation with similarities to certain types of human stimulus-response reactions.

Sections 4 and 5 are concerned with a more or less specifically defined device called a "perceptron". An attempt is made to define a perception-like automaton as a nerve-net (in the sense of Kleene [2] and von Neumann [3]). Although there are some difficulties in this formulation, due to vagueness and contradictions in the descriptions of perceptrons in [4], it seems clear that the proposed model has or can have all of the features of a perceptron which are claimed to be novel. It is then shown that such a device can be represented at any instant of time as a very special type of set function. Some questions regarding the possibility of solving the basic discrimination problem with these special set functions are then considered.

In Section 6 a concept is introduced which should prove useful in treating approximate discrimination problems.

It is believed that much of the material in this paper can be applied to automata constructed along the more con-

ventional lines of "McCollough-Pitts nerve nets." These
applications will be reported on in the future.

2. Stimuli, Responses and Discrimination Functions.

Procedures for the digitilization of various types of
information are so well known that we merely assert here
the assumption that whatever "knowledge" an automation is
to have of its external environment is in the form of a
finite bounded sequence of 0's and 1's (i.e. a binary
integer). Conceptually the device may be thought of as
having a finite number of input lines (sensors or input
neurons) which we may order in some arbitrary but fixed
manner. The input binary integer then represents stimulation of those input lines which correspond to a 1 and
non-stimulation of the others.

Similarly the digital control of servos and other
"active" control mechanisms is sufficiently developed to
enable us to limit the response of an automaton to finite
binary integers. The output lines (response units or
effectors) are assumed to be finite in number and are
stimulated or non-stimulated in accordance with the
appearance of a 1 or 0 in the corresponding position in
the binary integer. With these heuristic notions in mind
we introduce

Definition 2.1. A binary vector, x , of dimension n
is a (column) vector of n components, x_i , $i = 1, 2, \ldots, n$
each of which is either 0 or 1 .

Such binary vectors (or equivalently for some purposes,
binary integers) are the basic quantities in terms of which

the input, output and state of finite automata will be
described. The following facts concerning binary vectors
are elementary:

(i) The set of all n-dimensional binary vectors contains
2^n elements.

(ii) The number of non-zero components common to two
n-dimensional binary vectors, $\underset{\sim}{x}$ and $\underset{\sim}{y}$, is given by
their (real) inner product $(\underset{\sim}{x},\underset{\sim}{y}) = (\underset{\sim}{y},\underset{\sim}{x}) = \sum_{i=1}^{n} x_i y_i$.

Definition 2.2. Let j,k, and n be positive integers and

$$\left.\begin{array}{c} S \\ A \\ R \end{array}\right\} = \underline{\text{the set of all}} \left\{\begin{array}{c} n \\ j \\ k \end{array}\right\} \underline{\text{-dimensional binary vectors,}} \left\{\begin{array}{c} \underset{\sim}{s} \\ \underset{\sim}{a} \\ \underset{\sim}{r} \end{array}\right\}$$

Definition 2.3. $F(S,R)$ = the set of all single valued functions,

$$f(\underset{\sim}{s}) = \underset{\sim}{r} ,$$

on S to R ; i.e. with domain S and range in R .

The set S is to be considered the set of all possible
stimuli to an automaton with n-input lines. The set R
is the set of all possible responses of an automaton with
k-output lines. Any finite automaton with n-input lines
and k-output lines then corresponds to some function
$f \in F(S,R)$; i.e. F is equivalent to the set of all
such automata. If for any set X we let $\eta(X)$ be the
number of elements in the set the above definitions yield

$$\eta(F) = [\eta(R)]^{\eta(S)} = 2^{k \cdot 2n} . \qquad (2.0)$$

(8)

Definition 2.4. Let $S_1, S_2, \ldots, S_m$ be $m \geq 1$
disjoint subsets[1] of S , and

$$I_m \equiv \left\{ S_1, S_2, \ldots, S_m \right\} , \quad U_m \equiv S_1 \cup S_2 \ldots \cup S_m .$$

Let $r_1, r_2, \ldots, r_m$ be m distinct elements[2] of R , and

$$O_m \equiv \left\{ r_1, r_2, \ldots, r_m \right\} .$$

A) A function $f \in F(S, R)$ is a discrimination function
of I_m with respect to O_m if:

$$f(s) = r_\mu \quad \text{for all } s \in S_\mu , \mu = 1, 2, \ldots, m.$$

B) A function $f \in F(S, R)$ is a strong discrimination
function of I_m w.r.t. O_m if it is a discrimination
function of I_m w.r.t. O_m and in addition:

$$f(s) \neq r_\mu \quad \text{if } s \notin S_\mu , \mu = 1, 2, \ldots, m.$$

C) $F_D(I_m, O_m) \equiv$ the set of all discrimination functions of
I_m w.r.t. O_m .

D) $F_{str.D}(I_m, O_m) \equiv$ the set of all strong discrimination
functions of I_m w.r.t. O_m .

Clearly a large class, if not all, of the desired
overall properties of a finite automaton can be formulated
in terms of the above notions of discrimination functions.
Thus if a device is to respond in one way to one class of
inputs and in a different way to a second class of inputs,
etc., it must correspond precisely to a discrimination

function. It is perhaps not "natural", if we are trying
to imitate human behaviour to insist upon strong discrimination. This would imply that certain responses can be
caused only by certain known stimuli (i.e. all hallucinations
and illusions would have to be anticipated). However strong
discrimination functions seem to play an important role in
constructive existence proofs. (They are in fact the kinds
of set functions implied by Kleene [2] and von Neumann [3]
where, however, m is implicitly taken to be 2 and k = 1.
It would also seem that the class of problems more vaguely
formulated by F. Rosenblatt [4] are clarified by these
notions and again m = 1 or 2 in most of his explicit
discussions.)

The existence and uniqueness properties of discrimination functions (and hence the possible existence and
uniqueness of the implied class of automatons) are
contained in the following, essentially trivial, results.
It is assumed throughout this discussion that a definite
discrimination problem, characterized by I_m and O_m,
is posed.

Tr. 2.1. A discrimination function of I_m w.r.t. O_m
exist, if and only if $m \leq 2^k$.

Proof. From the definitions 2.2 and 2.4, since $O_m \subseteq R$,

$$m = \eta(O_m \leq \eta(R) = 2^k . \qquad (2.1)$$

Thus the necessity is established. The sufficiency is
obvious as the definition 2.4 then becomes essentially

(10)

constructive.[3]

Tr. 2.2   The following three statements are equivalent:

    (a)   A discrimination function of I_m w.r.t. O_m is unique.

    (b) $U_m = S$.

    (c) $F_D(I_m, O_m) = F_{str.D}(I_m, O_m)$.

Proof.   The equivalence between (a) and (b) follows from
"counting" the possible number of discrimination functions.
Since for all discrimination functions $f \in F_D(I_m, O_m)$,

$$f(U_m) = O_m ,$$

in an obvious notation, they can differ only in mapping
$(S-U_m)$ into R . The number of ways in which this can be
done, and hence the number of possible discrimination
functions, is

$$\eta (F_D) = [\eta (R)]^{\eta (S-U_m)} , \qquad (2.2)$$

    Similarly to show the equivalence between (b) and (c)
we count the strong discrimination functions,

$$\eta (F_{str.D}) = [\eta (R-O_m)]^{\eta (S-U_m)} , \qquad (2.3)$$

and the result follows on equating (2.2) and (2.3).   (Note
that the above proof relies on the condition $m \geq 1$
which was imposed in Defn. 2.4.   Kleene does not require
the equivalent of this condition [2] and is then forced to
consider the ensuing special trivial cases which correspond

(11)

to automata with no input or else no output.) The proof
is now complete.

   The above equation (2.3) and Tr. 2.2 clearly imply
the following result which has direct significance to the
analysis in [2] and [3] (since, as has been mentioned,
they take $m = 2$ and $k = 1$ which implies by (2.1) that
$R = O_m$) .

Tr. 2.3. If $R = O_m$ a strong discrimination function of
I_m w.r.t. O_m exists if and only if $S = U_m$, and it is
then unique.

   This result makes clear the possible difficulties and
care which must be taken in discussing general discrimination
problems while assuming $k = 1$ (i.e. only one output line
or effector). In fact if strong discrimination of only one
set $S' \ S$ is desired the problem is identical to that of
finding any discrimination function of $I_2 = \{S', S-S'\}$ w.r.t.
$O_2 = R$. Of course by Tr. 2.3 there is a unique such function.
Hence, speaking very loosely, it would seem unlikely, in
such cases, that an automaton constructed "mainly" by random
processes could yield the desired discrimination function.

   Finally to obtain some notion of the relative "density"
of F_D in F we have

Tr. 2.4. The probability that a function f chosen at
random from F be a discrimination function of I_m w.r.t. O_m
is

(12)

$$p(f \; \epsilon \; F_D) = 2^{-k\eta(U_m)} . \tag{2.4}$$

Proof. The probability in question is just the ratio $\eta(F_D)/\eta(F)$. Thus from (2.0), (2.2) and the fact that the S_μ are disjoint:

$$p(f \; \epsilon \; F_D) = \frac{[\eta(R)]^{\eta(S-U_m)}}{[\eta(R)]^{\eta(S)}} = \frac{[\eta(R)]^{\eta(S)-\eta(U_m)}}{[\eta(R)]^{\eta(S)}}$$

$$= [\eta(R)]^{-\eta(U_m)} = 2^{-k\eta(U_m)} .$$

This result exhibits the obvious fact that reducing k increases the probability of selecting a discrimination function at random, or equivalently, that it increases the relative density of them in F . Of course in any interesting case $\eta(U_m) \gg 1$ so a reduction in k may be of no great consequence in practical considerations.

3. A Pattern Recognizing Automaton.

We consider here a simple example which, while of interest in itself, may also aid in conceptually understanding some of the notions previously introduced. The example is concerned with the recognition, by some type of device, of a variety of geometric patterns (i.e. printed characters, etc.) Problems related to the study of such devices are frequently considered to belong to the field of finite automata.

One of the main features in this example is a clear description of how seemingly complicated (visual) information can be correlated with well defined subsets S_μ. In general the question of how these subsets differ, or rather what all the elements $\underset{\sim}{s} \; \varepsilon \; S_\mu$ of any particular subset have in common, is not directly related to the theoretical existence problems previously discussed. However, in any practical discrimination problem this question is really basic. A considerable part of the discussion in [4] seems to be concerned with just such matters.

We assume that the patterns to be recognized are displayed in the unit square, $\left\{ 0 \leq x \leq 1 \; ; \; 0 \leq y \leq 1 \right\}$, of the x-y plane. On this square we place a uniform grid $x_\alpha = \alpha h$, $y_\beta = \beta h$ of mesh size $h = \frac{1}{p}$ and so the integers α, β take on the values $0, 1, \ldots, p$. Thus the unit square is partitioned into p^2 elementary squares of side h. We now impose some very severe restrictions

on the patterns to be recognized and on how they are to be
displayed. Later we discuss the relaxation of these conditions.

G_1) Each pattern is composed of elementary squares.

G_2) Distinct patterns are composed of <u>different
numbers</u> of elementary squares.

G_3) When a pattern is displayed[4] its boundary must
coincide with segments of any of the grid lines
$x = x_\alpha$, $y = y_\beta$.

These restrictions imply that at most p^2 such
patterns can be defined.

Thinking of gadgetry for the moment a pattern may be
displayed in any admissible position by illuminating the
appropriate elementary squares. An automaton is imagined
which has p^2 input lines, one from each of the elementary
squares. Then by any of a variety of well-known scanning
techniques a unit signal can be made to appear on those
lines initiating from illuminated squares and no signal
will be present on the others. (In actual practice of
course a negative unit signal is usually used to indicate
no input. However, we do not wish to go into the details
of these technicalities and so will continue to use loose
terminology, as above, in describing hardware.) The
class of possible input signals is thus equivalent to the
set S of $n = p^2$ dimensional binary vectors.

(15)

Let the distinct patterns to be recognized be denoted by the symbols c_1, c_2, ..., c_m and let the integer N_μ be the number of elementary squares required to construct c_μ , $\mu = 1, 2, ..., m$. Then by G_2) we must have

$$N_\mu = N_\nu \quad \text{i.a.o.i.} \quad \mu = \nu .\qquad (3.0)$$

If any pattern c_μ is displayed in a definite position on the unit square in accordance with G_3), then a corresponding unique binary vector $\underset{\sim}{s} \; \varepsilon \; S$ can be defined which represents the resulting input to the automaton. The set of all such vectors which can be obtained from all admissible positions of c_μ is denoted by S_μ . This is to be done for all $\mu = 1, 2, ..., m$. Thus any admissible display of c_μ is represented by one and only one vector in S_μ and any admissible display of any of the patterns c_1 , c_2, ..., c_m is represented by one and only one vector in

$$U_m = S_1 \cup S_2 \; ... \; \cup S_m .$$

Furthermore by the property noted earlier of scalar products of binary vectors we have:

For all $\underset{\sim}{s} \; \varepsilon \; S_\mu$, $(\underset{\sim}{s}, \underset{\sim}{s}) = N_\mu$; $\mu = 1, 2, ..., m$.   (3.1)

This result and (3.0) imply that for any $\underset{\sim}{s}$ and $\underset{\sim}{s}'$ in U_m :

$$(\underset{\sim}{s},\underset{\sim}{s}) = (\underset{\sim}{s}',\underset{\sim}{s}') \quad \text{i.a.o.i.} \quad \underset{\sim}{s} \ \varepsilon \ S_\mu \ , \ \underset{\sim}{s}' \ \varepsilon \ S_\mu \qquad (3.2)$$

for some μ (i.e. they must be images of the same pattern).
Clearly then is this example the feature in common to all
$s \ \varepsilon \ S_\mu$ is their value of (s,s) . Of course it is
elementary that the area of any geometric pattern is in-
varient under all translations and rotations. We have
merely required, in G_2), that the patterns being considered
have unequal area. (In the above notation the area covered
by c_μ is simply $h^2 N_\mu$.) These considerations of area
form the basis for generalizing the present example to
much more complicated cases.

Returning to the proposed automaton we let all the
input lines go to some device which adds the binary
signals on them and represents the sum as a binary number.
(Such an adder is simply constructed and would require
$2 \log_2 p$ stages for the fastest series-parallel operation.
The adders in the k-th stage would have to add k-bit
binary integers in parallel and there would have to be
at most $2^{-k} p^2$ of them. Thus the maximum number of
adders required is $p^2 - 1$, for the fastest operation.)
The largest possible sum is p^2 and so the output signal
requires at most $2 \log_2 p$ binary bits or output lines.
If we let k be the smallest integer $\geq 2 \log_2 p$, then
any output can be represented by a k-dimensional binary
vector. The set R of all such vectors, $\underset{\sim}{r}$, is the
class of all possible responses of the automaton in

(17)

question. Let the vector which is the binary representation of the integer N_μ be denoted by $\underset{\sim}{r}_\mu$, $\mu = 1, 2, \ldots, m$. These vectors are clearly unique.

With the definitions

$$O_m \equiv \left\{ \underset{\sim}{r}_1, \underset{\sim}{r}_2, \ldots, \underset{\sim}{r}_m \right\} \quad , \quad I_m \equiv \left\{ s_1, s_2, \ldots, s_m \right\} \quad ,$$

we can now interpret the discrimination problems of I_m with respect to O_m : they are concerned with recognizing m patterns, c_μ , in various positions in the unit square. For this problem the automaton whose construction has been indicated above is a representation of some $f \in F_D(I_m, O_m)$. Thus the ordinary discrimination problem is solved and indeed the proposed device should be of practical significance.

However, strong discrimination is not possible with this automaton. Clearly some pattern, $c \not\equiv c_\mu$ of elementary squares can have the area $h^2 N_\mu$ and the corresponding signal $\underset{\sim}{s}$ is then in S_μ . So some patterns which are not c_μ will be identified as c_μ . Whether this situation is tolerable or not depends upon the intended use of the device and the total class of patterns to which it will be exposed.

We turn now to a consideration of the recognition of more general patterns than those of G_1) with greater freedom of display than in G_3). However, the essence of G_2) will be retained in a somewhat altered form. Again the

patterns are denoted by c_μ and they are to be displayed
in the unit square. We denote the area of c_μ by $A(c_\mu)$,
$\mu = 1,2, \ldots, m$. The shape of the c_μ can be quite
general (say with piecewise smooth boundaries) but we will
not go into any analytical details; the requirement that
$A(c_\mu)$ is well defined can be considered the condition
G_1') which replaces G_1). Condition G_2) is replaced by:

G_2') $|A(c_\mu)-A(c_\nu)| \geq \delta > 0$, $\mu \neq \nu$, $\mu,\nu = 1,2, \ldots, m$.

In other words the areas of the c_μ must differ by at
least δ , some fixed positive number.

There are no restrictions on how or where the c_μ
can be displayed in the unit square (and as in footnote 4
they may intersect the boundaries). However, we must now
require the mesh size h to be sufficiently small. To
specify this precisely we should know the exact conditions
of illumination under which a sensed elementary square will
emit a signal (i.e. if half the area is illuminated, etc.).
In any event let $N_\mu(h;x,y,\Theta)$ be the number of elementary
squares of side h that emit a signal when the image of
c_μ has, say, its centroid at x,y and some fixed axis
at an angle Θ with the positive x-axis. Then we require
h to be such that

G_3') $A(c_\mu) - \dfrac{\varepsilon}{2} \leq N_\mu(h;x,y,\Theta) \leq A(c_\mu) + \dfrac{\varepsilon}{2}$, $\left\{ \begin{array}{l} 0 \leq x,y, \leq 1 \\ 0 \leq \Theta \leq 2\pi \;\; ; \\ \mu = 1,2, \ldots, m \end{array} \right.$

for some fixed ε in $0 < \varepsilon < \delta$. That is, we require the "sensitized area" of any image of any c_μ to be "close" to the exact area. Close here means only less than half the difference between the two closest areas $A(c_\mu)$.

Now the input classes are defined such that:

$$\underset{\sim}{s} \ \varepsilon \ S_\mu \ \text{i.a.o.i.} \ A(c_\mu) - \frac{\varepsilon}{2} \leq (\underset{\sim}{s}, \underset{\sim}{s}) \leq A(c_\mu) + \frac{\varepsilon}{2} \ ; \qquad (3.3)$$

$$\mu = 1, 2, \ldots, m \ .$$

From conditions G_2') and G_3') it follows that these sets S_μ are disjoint.

The output or response classes of the automaton are now defined by means of the generalization described in footnote 2. If for any binary vector $\underset{\sim}{x}$ we let $N(\underset{\sim}{x})$ be the integer whose binary representation is given by $\underset{\sim}{x}$ then the response classes, R_μ , are defined by:

$$\underset{\sim}{r} \ \varepsilon \ R_\mu \ \text{i.a.o.i.} \ A(c_\mu) - \frac{\varepsilon}{2} \leq N(\underset{\sim}{r}) \leq A(c_\mu) + \frac{\varepsilon}{2} \ ; \qquad (3.4)$$

$$\mu = 1, 2, \ldots, m \ .$$

With the above definitions of S_μ and R_μ , and h taken to satisfy G_3'), the automaton previously described solves the ordinary discrimination problem for the very general patterns now allowed. Of course as before some spurious inputs may be recognized as patterns. But it should also be noted that now inexact representation of the patterns or even malfunctioning of a few of the inputs from elementary squares need not destroy proper recognition. The "amount" of error that can be tolerated is determined by ε and h for any given c_μ .

The practicality of such a general pattern recognizing automaton must depend upon the value of h required. Of course if the patterns in question have complicated shapes then small values of h are necessary for good resolution of the areas of the images. Similarly if two patterns have nearly equal area (i.e. small δ) then ε must be small and, regardless of the complexity of their shapes, h must again be small to satisfy G_3') for these patterns. The number of elementary squares required is $p^2 = \dfrac{1}{h^2}$ and the number of adders required has been shown to be at most p^2-1 . However, these adders are of unequal complexity but it is easily shown that they can all be composed of $p^2(p^2-1)$ basic units. Thus the total basic hardware required is of the order of $p^4 = \dfrac{1}{h^4}$ units. While these estimates lead to large numbers they indicate that meshes of the order of $h = 10^{-2}$ could be realized. If slower speeds are allowed, which seems quite reasonable, the hardware can be greatly reduced by the use of simple counters and appropriate time delays.

4. "Perceptron"-like Automata.

The discussion of Section 2 is so general that (with the inclusion of time delays, which are considered briefly in Section 7) it applies to most finite automata. In the sense of that discussion two automata are completely equivalent if they correspond to the same set function $f \varepsilon F$. However there remain a number of important questions:

(1) Can an automaton be constructed according to some definite rules and represent any discrimination function $f \varepsilon F_D$ of a given discrimination problem?

(2) Can, instead, an automaton be constructed which will approximate sufficiently closely any $f \varepsilon F_D$, in some appropriate norm?

In the fundamental papers of Kleene [2] and von Neumann [3] it is shown that these questions can be answered in the affirmative. More particularly, for a specific class of discrimination problems, Kleene characterizes all those $F_{str.D}$ for which an equivalent automaton of a specified construction exists. von Neumann shows the existence for some $F_{str.D}$ of automata constructed in a slightly different manner. His main concern, however, is with a thorough analysis of the second question using a "probabilistic" norm (while the basic units of which the automaton is constructed are not assumed to function perfectly)! Also in the previous section a particular automaton is described which represents a variety of specific discrimination functions. In the light of these results it would seem advisable for any proposed automaton to first study the existence or approximation problems.

A specific class of automata is defined by specifying the basic elements of which it is to be composed together with rules for their combination or connection. This is done in complete detail for a variety of such automata in [1,2,3] and more vaguely in Section 2. The basic elements are usually called "neurons" and a collection of them formed into an automaton by the prescribed rules of connection form a "nerve net". By selecting a particular adder such a description is easily given for the pattern recognizing automaton. We shall try to develope such a formulation for an even more vaguely proposed automaton referred to as a "perceptron" in [4]. The "nerve net" to be introduced may not have all of the properties mentioned in [4] but it is believed that most of the excluded properties are more restrictive. Hence the proposed model should include as special cases various types of "perceptrons".

The S-units: In [4] basic units are introduced which essentially describe the binary nature of the input signals to an automaton. The only concern with such units need be in discussions of the digitalization of various kinds of "information". Since we assume such techniques known these input units are really superfluous. However, if it

(23)

aids conceptually one may think of an S-unit as having
only two possible states: stimulated and non-stimulated
(as an example we may think of the elementary squares).
From each such unit eminates one output line (wire or nerve
fiber). If an S-unit is stimulated at time t , a unit
signal is instantaneously transmitted on its output line.

If there are n such S-units in a given automaton
they can be ordered in some arbitrary but fixed manner.
Then the "state" of all the S-units at any instant can be
represented by some n-dimensional binary vector, $\underset{\sim}{s} \in S$.
(The symbol S always represents the set in Defn. 2.2.
The combination "S-unit" has the meaning implied above
and should cause no confusion.) Thus S is the set of
all possible states of the S-units of the automaton in
question.

The Generalized A-units: This unit is a modification of
one of the special "neuron" models used in [1] and [3].
A schematic diagram of the A-unit is presented in Figure 1.
It has one output line and some positive finite number of
input lines. The input lines are attached to the A-unit
by one of three types of connections[5]: "e" or excitatory;
"i", or inhibitory; "c", or value changing. Each of the
input lines can be either stimulated or non-stimulated and
in the former state they instantaneously transmit a unit
signal to the A-unit through the appropriate type of
connection. The A-unit itself is stimulated if

(24)

$$n_e - n_i \geq \Theta \;, \tag{4.0}$$

and non-stimulated otherwise. Here n_e and n_i are the number of stimulated "e" and "i" input lines, respectively, and Θ is a fixed positive <u>constant</u> called the threshold. (We note here immediately that non-integral values of Θ are superfluous since (4.0) implies that the state of an A-unit is a piecewise constant function[6] of Θ .) If the A-unit is stimulated at time t it transmits a signal, at time $t+\delta_A$, on the output line. However, this signal need not be a unit signal but has associated with it a "value",[7] $v(t+\delta_A)$, say amplitude of the signal, which is a function of $v(t)$ and $n_c(t)$, the number of "c" input lines stimulated at time t. The time lag, δ_A , is a fixed non-negative quantity (see further discussion).

If there are j such A-units in a given automaton they can be ordered in some arbitrary but fixed manner. Then the "state with regard to stimulation" of all the A-units at any instant, t , can be represented by some j-dimensional binary vector, say $\underset{\sim}{a}(t) \in A$ (1 corresponding to stimulation and 0 otherwise). Thus the set A of Defn. 2.2 represents the set of all possible states of stimulation of the A-units at any instant.

Let the diagonal square matrix of order j,

$$V(t) \equiv (\delta_{\alpha,\beta} v_\beta(t)) \tag{4.1}$$

(25)

contain as β-th diagonal entry the value, $v_\beta(t)$, of
the β-th A-unit (according to the above implied ordering)
at time t . Then the j-dimensional vector

$$V(t+\delta_A) \; a(t) \qquad\qquad (4.2)$$

represents the state, with regard to value, of the output
lines of all the A-units at time $t+\delta_A$. (The form of
functional dependence of $v(t+\delta_A)$ on $v(t)$ and $n_c(t)$
will be shown later to be superfluous for our purpose.)
The R-units: A schematic diagram of an R-unit is presented
in Figure 2. It has one output line and any positive finite
number of input lines. The input lines are connected to
one of two types of connections, "e" or "i" . Each
input line is either stimulated or non-stimulated and only
in the former case they instantaneously transmit a signal
to the R-unit through the appropriate connection. However,
these input signals need not be unit-signals but have the
value (magnitude) v carried by the corresponding input
line. The R-unit will be stimulated if the sum of the
values of the stimulated "e" input lines minus the sum
of the values of the stimulated "i" input lines is $\geq \theta'$.
Otherwise the R-unit is non-stimulated. That is if $v_a(t)$,
$a = a_1, a_2, \ldots, a_q$ are the values on the q input lines
to a given R-unit, then it is stimulated if[8]

$$\sum_{q'=1}^{q} y_{a_{q'}} \; v_{a_{q'}} \quad (t) \geq \theta' \; , \qquad (4.3)$$

(26)

where $y_{\alpha_{q'}} = +1$ or -1 according as the $\alpha_{q'}$-th input line is of connection type "e" or "i" , respectively. If an R-unit is stimulated at time t it transmits a unit signal on the output line at time $t+h(t)$. The time lag, $h(t)$, is to be a function of the values, $v_\alpha(t)$, of those input lines which are stimulated at time t . This time lag will be dispensed with later.[9]

If there are k such R-units in a given automaton then, as with the S-units and A-units, the set R of Defn. 2.2 represents all possible states of stimulation of the R-units. Any binary vector $\underset{\sim}{r} \, \epsilon \, R$ is a possible "state" of all the R-units at any instant t (and similarly represents a possible state of the output lines of all R-units at any instant).

The General Perceptron "Nerve-net": Rules for the combination of the three basic units and the application of inputs (or stimulation and non-stimulation) to the S-units determine a general nerve-net, automaton or perception-like device. These rules, insofar as we can determine them from [4], are as follows (with some possibly trivial but necessary modifications and additions of our own):

(i) The output line from any basic unit can be divided into any finite number of branches each transmitting the identical signal initiated by that unit.

(ii) The output branches from an S-unit must be connected to the "e" or "i" inputs of an A-unit. At most one

(27)

such branch from any S-unit can be connected to any A-unit.
Every S-unit must be connected to at least one A-unit.

(iii) The output branches from an A-unit must be connected
to the inputs of an R-unit, with at most one such branch
from any A-unit to any R-unit, and at least one such
connection from each A-unit.

(iv) The output branches from an R-unit may be connected
to the "c" input of an A-unit.

(v) Signals to the S-units are to be applied at successive
instants of time, $t_o, t_o+\delta_s, t_o+2\delta_s, \ldots, t$ for _finite_
sequences of intervals.

The above rules and the previous definitions indicate
that there are still some missing rules or information.
In particular the possible time delays δ_s, δ_A, and h(t)
should probably all be integral multiples of some unit
interval for any reasonably functioning and understandable
non-analogue device. Furthermore, depending upon the type
of behaviour desired with respect to the past history (i.e.
"static" or "dynamic" memory effects) δ_s should be greater
than $\delta_A+h(t)$ or not. In the former case the entire
memory effect resides in the values, $v_j(t)$, while in
the latter case more complicated effects are possible.
It would seem for most considerations in [4] that the
assumption

$$\delta_s > \delta_A + \max_t h(t) \qquad\qquad (4.4)$$

(28)

is all that is required, and so we shall adopt it. (In
[2] and [3] a more complicated case is considered.)

An important limitation imposed by the rules (ii)-(iv)
is that such an automaton is incapable of counting or,
what is essentially equivalent, there can be no "closed"
active loops which transmit a signal periodically, say
with fixed period δ_A . These properties would become
possible if outputs of A-units or R-units were permitted
to be "e" and "i" inputs of A-units. (The "logical
depth", in the sense of [2] and [3], of the current automata
are then rather restricted.) In this regard there seems
to be some confusion in [4] where the verbal rules for
connections between basic units, pp. 25-27 et.seq., con-
tradict various diagrams, Figs. 1, 2b, 3, et.seq. However,
the extra connections allowed in the diagrams, from
R-units to R-units or A-units and from A-units to A-units,
are all "inhibitory" and thus would still not yield the
desired additional features mentioned above.

There are further restrictions imposed on the nets
considered in [4]. These will be dismissed later.

Using the notions of binary vector, etc., we may now
formulate a (mathematical) model of the proposed automaton.
The "input" to the automaton at any instant t is repre-
sented by a vector $\underset{\sim}{s}(t)$ ε S . The total resultant input
to the α-th A-unit at time t can then be represented by
the inner product

$$(\underset{\sim}{w}_\alpha \, , \, \underset{\sim}{s}(t))$$

where w_α is an n-component row vector whose components
are $0, \pm 1$ according to the rule:

$$\underset{\sim}{w}_\alpha \equiv (w_{\alpha,1} \, , \, w_{\alpha,2} \, , \, \ldots, \, w_{\alpha,n})$$

$$w_{\alpha,\beta} = \begin{cases} 0 & \text{if no output branch from the } \beta\text{-th input} \\ & \quad \text{goes to the } \alpha\text{-th A-unit;} \\ +1 & \text{if an output branch from the } \beta\text{-th input} \quad (4.5)\ (a) \\ & \quad \text{goes to an "e" input of the } \alpha\text{-th A-unit;} \\ -1 & \text{if an output branch from the } \beta\text{-th input} \\ & \quad \text{goes to an "i" input of the } \alpha\text{-th A-unit.} \end{cases}$$

Then forming the j-rowed by n-columned rectangular matrix

$$W \equiv (w_{\alpha,\beta}) \equiv \begin{pmatrix} \underset{\sim}{w}_1 \\ \underset{\sim}{w}_2 \\ \cdot \\ \cdot \\ \cdot \\ \underset{\sim}{w}_j \end{pmatrix} \, , \qquad (4.5)\ (b)$$

the inputs to all A-units at time t are given by

$$W \, \underset{\sim}{s}(t) \, .$$

To denote the state of stimulation of the A-units at
time t we introduce a threshold function which maps any
real finite dimensional vector into a binary vector of
the same dimension. Thus if x is a p-dimensional real
vector

(30)

$$T_\Theta(\underset{\sim}{x}) = \underset{\sim}{y} \;, \quad y_a = \begin{cases} 0 \;, & \text{if } x_a < \Theta \\[2mm] 1 \;, & \text{if } x_a \geq 0 \end{cases} \;, \quad a = 1, 2, \ldots, p. \quad (4.6)$$

Then the state of stimulation of all the A-units at time t is given by:

$$\underset{\sim}{a}(t) = T_\Theta(W \underset{\sim}{s}(t)) \;. \qquad (4.7)$$

Here, or course, $\underset{\sim}{a}(t) \; \varepsilon \; A$ and (4.7) represents a single valued function on S to A .

Assuming, for the present, that the values of all A-units at time t , the stimulated "c" input lines to all A-units at time t , and the rule for determining the values at $t + \delta_A$ are known we form, using (4.1), (4.2) and (4.7):

$$V(t + \delta_A) \; T_\Theta(W \underset{\sim}{s}(t)) \;. \qquad (4.8)$$

This a dimensional vector represents the state of the output lines of all A-units at time $t + \delta_A$. Now the inputs to all R-units at this time can be expressed by introducing the matrix Y , analogous to W :

$$Y = (y_{a, \beta}) \qquad (4.9)$$

$$y_{a, \beta} \equiv \begin{cases} 0 \text{ if no output branch from the } \beta^{th} \text{ A-unit} \\ \quad \text{goes to the } a^{th} \text{ R-unit;} \\[2mm] +1 \text{ if an output branch from the } \beta^{th} \text{ A-unit} \\ \quad \text{goes to an "e" input of the } a^{th} \\ \quad \text{R-unit;} \\[2mm] -1 \text{ if an output branch from the } \beta^{th} \text{ A-unit} \\ \quad \text{goes to an "i" input of the } a^{th} \text{ R-unit ;} \end{cases}$$

(31)

Using (4.8), (4.9) and the threshold function we finally
define

$$\underset{\sim}{r}(t+\delta_A) = T_{\Theta'} \left[Y \; V \; (t+\delta_A) \; T_{\Theta}[W \; \underset{\sim}{s}(t)] \right] \quad . \qquad (4.10)$$

This is a k-dimensional binary vector which represents
the state with regard to stimulation of all the R-units
at time $t+\delta_A$. Thus assuming we know how to evaluate
$V(t+\delta_A)$, the explicit expression (4.10) determines which
of the R-units are about to transmit signals and which
not. Furthermore the above expression represents a single
valued function on S to R and thus must be some $f \; \varepsilon \; F$.
Which particular function it represents at any instant
depends on the specification of the connections W, Y and
some as yet unrepresented ones, (the c inputs), the
thresholds Θ and Θ' , the rules for computing values
and perhaps time lags $h(t)$, <u>the past history of inputs</u>
$\underset{\sim}{s}(t_o)$, $\underset{\sim}{s}(t_o+\delta_s)$, ..., $\underset{\sim}{s}(t-\delta_s)$ <u>and initial state of the</u>
<u>values,</u> $V(t_o)$. In spite of this seeming complexity if
some input signal $\underset{\sim}{s} \; \varepsilon \; S$ at time t is to be mapped
into some response signal $\underset{\sim}{r} \; \varepsilon \; R$ at any time $t+\delta_A+h(t+\delta_A)$,
for any past history, by the above type of automaton then
there must exist (constant) quantities, Y, V, W, Θ and Θ'
such that

$$\underset{\sim}{r} = T_{\Theta'} \left[Y \; V \; T_{\Theta}[W \; \underset{\sim}{s}] \right] \qquad (4.11)$$

Furthermore if for some $t+\delta_A+h(t+\delta_A)$, as is implied by

(32)

the so-called "learning experiments" in [4], the automaton
is to be able to give the same response, say $\underset{\sim}{r}_1$, to
any $\underset{\sim}{s} \; \varepsilon \; S_1 \subset S$, then (4.11) must represent a discrimination
function of $I_1 = \left\{S_1\right\}$ with respect to $O_1 = \left\{\underset{\sim}{r}_1\right\}$. In
fact discrimination with respect to two sets is usually
discussed in [4] and the implications are that an arbitrary
finite number could be used. Thus if this is ever to be
possible it must be proven that there exist discrimination
functions of the form (4.11). This is trivial and is done
in the next section. The more difficult and interesting
task however would be to prove that some particular discrimination function can have this form.[10] Once such
results were obtained it would become reasonable to in-
vestigate the seemingly still more difficult problem of
the existence of "learning sequences", $\underset{\sim}{s}(t_o)$, $\underset{\sim}{s}(t_o + \delta_s)$,
..., $\underset{\sim}{s}(t - \delta_s)$ which would produce the desired discrimination
function.

Some of the properties of the operation of the automaton have been neglected in the above discussion; in
particular the delayed response of the R-units. However,
it is clear that such considerations do not add any new
"degrees of freedom" to the representation (4.10) since
only those R-units stimulated at time $t + \delta_A$ may transmit
signals later. Also the specific nature of the value
change cannot alter the discussion concerning (4.11).
These features are no doubt related to the problems con-

(33)

cerning "learning sequences" since they embody all the
memory aspects of the device.

In [4] there are many additional restrictions placed
on the net, i.e. "randomness" of various connecting lines,
equality of all thresholds, same number of "e" and "i"
inputs to each A-unit, and perhaps more. But again these
conditions can only restrict the generality formulated
above and possibly simplify some analysis. Hence we
shall not bother with these details in the present discussion.

5. Some Necessary Conditions for Discrimination by Perceptron-Like Automata.

It was shown in the previous section that in order for a perceptron-like automaton to represent a discrimination function, a function of the form

$$\underline{r} = T_{\Theta'}\left[Y \vee T_{\Theta}[W \underline{s}]\right] \equiv b(\underline{s}) \tag{5.0}$$

must also be able to represent a discrimination function. In this section we consider only functions of this form[11], (5.0), where, to summarize:

(a) $\underline{s} \in S$, $\underline{r} \in R$;

(b)
$$\left.\begin{array}{l} W \equiv (w_{a,\beta}) \ , \ w_{a,\beta} = 0, \pm 1 \\[4pt] Y \equiv (y_{\gamma,a}) \ , \ y_{\gamma,a} = 0, \pm 1 \\[4pt] V \equiv (v_a \delta_{\beta,a}) \ , \ v_a = \text{arb. real} \\ \hspace{5.5cm} \text{nos.} \end{array}\right\} \quad \left\{\begin{array}{l} \beta = 1, 2, \ldots, n \\ a = 1, 2, \ldots, j \\ \gamma = 1, 2, \ldots, k \end{array}\right. \tag{5.1}$$

(c) $\Theta, \Theta' > 0$, $T_{\Theta}(\underline{x}) = \underline{y}$, $y_\nu = \begin{cases} 0 \ , & \text{if } x_\nu < \Theta \\[4pt] 1 \ , & \text{if } y_\nu \geq \Theta \ . \end{cases}$

Thus it is easily shown that (5.0 - 1) defines a single valued function on S to R . Furthermore this function may be considered a "product" of two functions

$$b(\underline{s}) = h(g(\underline{s})) \ , \qquad \left\{\begin{array}{l} g(\underline{s}) \equiv T_{\Theta}[W \underline{s}] \\[12pt] h(\underline{a}) \equiv T_{\Theta'}[Y V \underline{a}] \ . \end{array}\right. \tag{5.2}$$

The function g is single valued on S to A and the

(35)

function h is single valued on A to R.

Definition 5.1. B = {the set of all function b($\underset{\sim}{s}$) of the form (5.0 - .2) on S to R} .

The set B is thus obtained by considering all possible "connections", W (from S-units to A-units) and Y (from A-units to R-units), all possible values, V , of A-units, and all possible positive thresholds Θ and Θ' . Thus every possible "state" of a perceptron at any instant can be represented by some function b ϵ B .

From the positivity assumption, (5.1c), on the thresholds it follows that for all b ϵ B :

$$b(\underset{\sim}{\emptyset}_S) = \underset{\sim}{\emptyset}_R \qquad (5.3)$$

where the null vectors, $\underset{\sim}{\emptyset}$, are to belong to the appropriate sets S and R . Thus we have

Tr. 5.1. B is a proper subset of F .

Proof. That B $\subseteq$ F follows from the definition (5.0 - .1); i.e. each b ϵ B is a single valued function on S to R and hence b ϵ F . B $\neq$ F follows from (5.3) and that B is not empty is obvious.

This result, though trivial, clearly indicates that perceptron-like automata cannot represent all functions on S to R . Another trivial though unfortunately relatively useless result is contained in

Tr. 5.2. For every b ϵ B there exist an integer $m \leq 2^k$ and sets I_m and O_m such that b ϵ $F_D(I_m, O_m)$. (In fact

the same is true for all $f \in F$.) The proof is obvious.
However, this result might give some hope for finding
"useful" discrimination functions in B . We turn to this
question now.

Definition 5.2. Let $g(\underset{\sim}{s})$ and $h(\underset{\sim}{a})$ be any two functions
of the form (5.2). Then $A_g(S') = \{$all $\underset{\sim}{a} \in A$ such that
$\underset{\sim}{a} = g(s)$ for some $\underset{\sim}{s} \in S' \subseteq S\}$;

$R_h(A') = \{$all $\underset{\sim}{r} \in R$ such that $\underset{\sim}{r} = h(a)$ for some
$\underset{\sim}{a} \in A' \subseteq A\}$. (That is, $A_g(S')$ is the image in A of
S' and $R_h(A')$ is the image in R of A' .)

From the above definition it is clear that, since g
and h are single valued,

$$\eta(A_g(S')) \leq \eta(S') \leq \eta(S) = 2^n$$
$$\eta(R_h(A')) \leq \eta(A') \leq \eta(A) = 2^j \quad .$$

(5.4)

Then for any given discrimination problem, characterized
by some set $F_D(I_m, O_m)$, we have

Tr. 5.3. A necessary condition that $F_D(I_m, O_m) \cap B \neq \emptyset$
(i.e. that B contain a discrimination function of I_m
w.r.t. O_m) is $2^j \geq m$.

Proof. From (5.2) and (5.4) it follows that $\eta(R_h(A)) \leq 2^j$
for all h and hence for all $b \in B$. But $\eta(O_m) = m$
and the proof is complete.

This result indicates that there must be at least
$(\log_2 m)$ A-units in any perceptron which is to discriminate
between m sets of stimuli. (It is suggested in [4] that

many A-units should be used but, since $m = 1$ or 2 in most discussions there, the required condition of Tr. 5.3 is easily satisfied with relatively few A-units. However, see the discussion after Tr. 5.5.)

Tr. 5.4. A necessary condition that $F_D(I_m O_m) \cap B \neq \emptyset$ is that either $\underset{\sim}{\emptyset}_S \not\in U_m$ or else $f(\underset{\sim}{\emptyset}_S) = \underset{\sim}{\emptyset}_R$ for some $f \in F_D$.

Proof. Obvious from (5.3).

This condition seems to be completely disregarded or unsuspected in [4]. On the other hand kleene [2] carefully distinguishes so-called "positive definite events" which essentially require $\underset{\sim}{\emptyset}_S \not\in U_m$. Thus a result of the above form is relevant to various kinds of automata, not only those described by the set B .

Tr. 5.5. A necessary condition that $F_D(I_m, O_m) \cap B \neq \emptyset$ is that for some function g , defined in (5.2) ,

$$A_g(S_\mu) \cap A_g(S_\nu) = \emptyset \text{ for all } \mu, \nu \text{ such that } \mu \neq \nu . \quad (5.5)$$

Proof. Since every $b \in B$ is of the form $b = h(g)$, by (5.2), for any $b \in F_D(I_m, O_m)$ there must exist h and g such that:

$$R_h(A_g(S_\mu)) = \underset{\sim}{r}_\mu , \qquad \mu = 1, 2, \ldots, m .$$

However, the functions h are single valued and so the sets $A_g(S_\mu)$ must be pairwise disjoint (we recall that the elements $\underset{\sim}{r}_\mu$ are distinct). This concludes the proof.

(38)

There is some discussion on page 41 of [4] which may
have relevance to the above condition. In fact the state-
ment "No restraints are placed on S(-unit) connections ..."
would seem to directly violate the implications of Tr. 5.5.
If we assume "random" connections from S-units to A-units,
subject to the restrictions on page 41 of [4], it should
not be too difficult to calculate the probability of
violating (5.5). It is not clear that this probability
can be made negligibly small for "practical" parameter
values, but again, requiring a "large" number of A-units,
as is suggested in [4], is a step in the right direction.

6. Approximate Discrimination.

In mechanisms of the complexity implied by the usual
concepts of automata it is perhaps unreasonable to require
that a proposed automation _exactly_ represent a given
discrimination class, $F_D(I_m, O_m)$. The most obvious reason
is the possible malfunctioning of the basic units, of which
there are assumed to be very many ($\approx 10^{10}$ for human
systems). This type of difficulty has been investigated by
von Neumann [3] and, in principle, he has shown that
"reliable" systems (with an arbitrarily small probability
of error in strong discrimination) can be constructed for
a particular type of nerve-net and discrimination problem.
However, it seems reasonable not to expect exact discrimination
on another (not unrelated) basis. This is, roughly, that
in analogy with human systems two stimuli in the same class,
say S_μ , could have responses that are "close" to each
other but not necessarily identical (as in Section 3 where
generalized discrimination was used to avoid this difficulty.)
These notions can be made precise by introducing some
measure of the "distance" of any function $f \in F$ from the
set $F_D(I_m, O_m) \subset F$.

Definition 6.1. For any discrimination class $F_D(I_m, O_m)$
we assign a real number, $\|f\|_D$, to each $f \in F$ by:

$$\|f\|_D \equiv \frac{1}{m} \sum_{\mu=1}^{m} \sum_{\underset{\sim}{s} \in S_\mu} \frac{(f(\underset{\sim}{s}) - \underset{\sim}{r}_\mu, f(\underset{\sim}{s}) - \underset{\sim}{r}_\mu)}{k \eta (S_\mu)} . \tag{6.0}$$

Clearly $\|f\|_D = 0$ if and only if $f \, \varepsilon \, F_D$. The maximum value of $(f(\underset{\sim}{s}) - \underset{\sim}{r}_\mu \, , \, f(\underset{\sim}{s}) - \underset{\sim}{r}_\mu)$ is k , which occurs if and only if each component is ± 1 . This implies that $f(\underset{\sim}{s})$ is the "complement" of $\underset{\sim}{r}_\mu$ with respect to the component values $0, 1$; or in obvious terminology "$f(\underset{\sim}{s})$ is as different from $\underset{\sim}{r}_\mu$ as possible". If for each $\underset{\sim}{s} \subset U_m$, $f(\underset{\sim}{s})$ is as different from the corresponding $\underset{\sim}{r}_\mu$ as possible then $\|f\|_D = 1$. These results are summarized in

Tr. 6.1. For any $F_D(I_m, O_m)$ and all $f \, \varepsilon \, F$,

$$0 \le \|f\|_D \le 1 \, .$$

$\|f\|_D = 0$ i.a.o.i. $f \, \varepsilon \, F_D$. If $\|f\|_D = 1$ then $f(\underset{\sim}{s}) = \underset{\sim}{1} - \underset{\sim}{r}_\mu$ for all $\underset{\sim}{s} \, \varepsilon \, S_\mu$, $\mu = 1, 2, \ldots, m$; where $\underset{\sim}{1} = (1, 1, \ldots, 1)^T$

To see how this measure of distance may be used in requiring close approximations, or to see just how small values of $\|f\|_D$ must be for some desired degree of approximation we note

Tr. 6.2. (a) If

$$\|f\|_D < \frac{1}{k}$$

then $f(\underset{\sim}{s}) = \underset{\sim}{r}_\mu$ for at least one $\mu = 1, 2, \ldots, m$ and at least one $\underset{\sim}{s} \, \varepsilon \, S_\mu$.

(b) If

$$\|f\|_D < [\frac{1}{k \cdot m \cdot \max_\mu \, \eta(S_\mu)}] \equiv \varepsilon_o$$

(41)

then $\|f\|_D = 0$ <u>and</u> $f \in F_D$.

<u>Proof</u>. For part (a) consider a function f which "misses" being a discrimination function by just one "bit" for every $\underset{\sim}{s} \in U_m$. For part (b) consider an f which "misses" by just one bit for only one $\underset{\sim}{s} \in U_m$. The proof then becomes clear.

The kind of probabilistic problems which should now be investigated are to find conditions such that: the <u>probability that</u> $\|f\|_D < \epsilon$, <u>can be made arbitrarily small</u>. This includes and generalizes the problems treated in [3] (where $\epsilon \leq \epsilon_o$) and the hope is that more practical automata can be found for reasonable values $\epsilon > \epsilon_o$.

7. Finite Discrete Time Sequences.

In most automata it is assumed that a temporal sequence of signals is to be applied and that a corresponding sequence of responses then follows. If we assume that the functioning of the device and the input of signals can be adequately described by considering only finite discrete sets of instants of time then our previous model is easily extended to include such situations.

So let us assume that the only instants at which the input signals and state of the automaton (including the output signals) need be specified is the set

$$T \equiv \left\{ t_1, t_2, \ldots, t_i \right\} . \qquad (7.0)$$

Of course we assume $t_{\tau+1} > t_\tau$ and, although not required here, it is also convenient to assume $t_{\tau+1} = t_1 + \tau \Delta t$, $\tau = 0, 1, 2, \ldots, i-1$. The sets S and R are those of Definition 2.2 and the automaton has n input lines and k output lines.

The input for the entire set T now consists of a set of i binary vectors $\underset{\sim}{s} \in S$. We may write any such total input set as a binary vector of dimension ni, say

$$\underset{=}{\overline{s}} \equiv \begin{pmatrix} \underset{\sim}{s}(t_1) \\ \underset{\sim}{s}(t_2) \\ \vdots \\ \underset{\sim}{s}(t_i) \end{pmatrix} \qquad (7.1)$$

(43)

Similarly the response for the set T is a binary vector
of dimension ki , say

$$\bar{\underset{\sim}{r}} \equiv \begin{pmatrix} \underset{\sim}{r}(t_1) \\ \underset{\sim}{r}(t_2) \\ \circ \\ \circ \\ \circ \\ \circ \\ \underset{\sim}{r}(t_i) \end{pmatrix} \circ \qquad (7.2)$$

The procedure is now clear: we define the sets

$$\left.\begin{matrix} \bar{S} \\ \\ \bar{R} \end{matrix}\right\} \equiv \text{ the set of all } \left\{\begin{matrix} N = ni \\ \\ K = ki \end{matrix}\right\} - \text{ dimensional binary vectors}\left\{\begin{matrix} \bar{\underset{\sim}{s}} \\ \\ \bar{\underset{\sim}{r}} \end{matrix}\right. \circ$$

Similarly corresponding set functions and discrimination
problems are defined in exact analogy to those of Section 2.
The results of that section then apply with only the
appropriate change in notation.

In order to use the present generalized model to
analize an automaton we would have to know precisely the
time delays in all of the units of that automaton. Thus
at the present we cannot apply it to perceptrons. However,
the automata described in [2] and [3], when restricted to
finite bounded time sequences T , are easily represented
as functions on $\bar{S}$ to $\bar{R}$.

(44)

FOOTNOTES

1. A single subset, S_μ , is called a definite event by
   Kleene. Thus we consider here the more general problem
   of distinguishing between m events, but in the more
   restrictive sense of neglecting time delays.

2. A useful generalization of these notions is obtained by
   replacing the $\underset{\sim}{r}_\mu$ by disjoint sets $R_\mu \subset R$. Then with
   the introduction of $V_m \equiv R_1 \cup R_2 \ldots \cup R_m$, results
   analogous to all of the following are easily stated and
   and proved. The R_μ are to be considered as sets of
   equivalent responses. With this generalization any
   strong discrimination problem of order m can be shown
   to be equivalent to an ordinary discrimination problem
   of order at most m+1.

3. For fixed n it is quite clear that there exists a k ,
   sufficiently large, such that discrimination functions
   exist for all I_m and O_m with $m \leq 2^{2^n}$. The
   arithmetic of this construction and some rather fanci-
   ful implications of it are contained in [5].

4. Notice that patterns may only be rotated by integral
   multiples of $\pi/2$. Translations may be allowed to
   carry a pattern across the boundary of the unit square
   if we require the same translation to be applied to
   replicas of the pattern in all neighboring unit squares.

(45)

Thus the part lost say in $x > 1$, is returned from $x < 0$.

In [4] the input signals themselves are said to be either "e" or "i" . This seems to be an unnecessary complication and is at variance with the types of signals transmitted in digital devices.

This observation indicates that the graphs in Figs. 5a, 5b, 11 (and perhaps others) of [4] cannot be correct; they must at least be step functions.

The notion of value distinguishes these A-units from the special neurons of [1] and [3]. However, if v can have only a finite set of values, say $\leq 2^q$ of them, the A-units could be constructed of q much simpler, "single-output" units (see [2] and [3]).

It is implied in this expression that $v_a(t) = 0$ if the a-th input line is not stimulated. This is clarified later in the complete model of the total nerve-net.

It should be mentioned that neurons with variable discrete time lags, depending upon the inputs, are briefly suggested in [2] and [3]. It would seem that such units can also be composed of the simpler basic units discussed in these papers.

Such problems are considered, for different automata, in

[2] and [3].

11. All the results of this section are much more general
and apply for arbitrary real matrices W, Y and V of
the indicated orders.

REFERENCES

[1] McCulloch, W.S. and Pitts, W., A logical calculus of
     the ideas imminent in nervous activity. Bull. Math.
     Biophys. 5 (1943), pp. 115-133.

[2] Kleene, S.C., Representation of events in nerve nets
     and finite automata. Automata Studies, Princeton Univ.
     Press (1956), pp. 3-41.

[3] von Neumann, J., Probabilistic logics and the synthesis
     of reliable organisms from unreliable components.
     Automata Studies, Princeton Univ. Press (1956),
     pp. 43-98.

[4] Rosenblatt, F., (a) The perceptron: a theory of
     statistical separability in cognitive systems. Cornell
     Aero. Lab., Inc., Report No. VG-1196-G-1 (1958).
                (b) Two theorems of statistical
     separability in the perceptron. Cornell Aero. Lab.,
     Inc., Report No. VG-1196-G-2 (1958).

[5] Culbertson, J.T., Some uneconomical robots, Automata
     Studies, Princeton Univ. Press (1956), pp. 99-116.

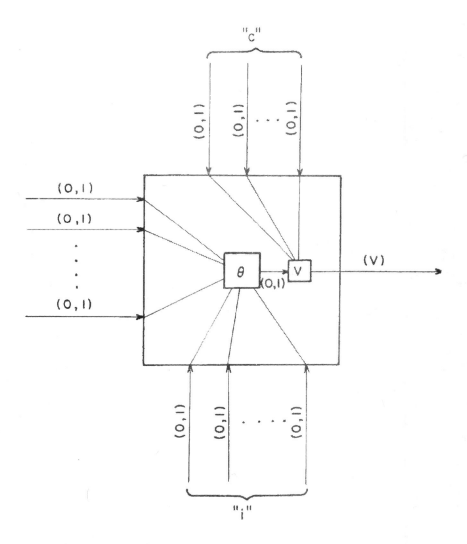

Figure I: Schematic diagram of an A-unit.

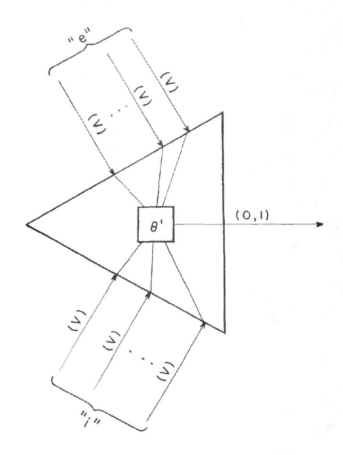

Figure 2: Schematic diagram of a R-unit.

(50)